ANOTHER DAY IN LANDOUR

Other Books by Ruskin Bond

Build Your English Skills with Ruskin Bond
How to Be a Writer
These Are a Few of My Favourite Things
Koki's Song
How to Live Your Life
The Enchanted Cottage
Zindagi Kaise Jiyen
The Golden Years

ANOTHER DAY IN LANDOUR

LOOKING OUT FROM MY WINDOW

RUSKIN BOND

HarperCollins *Publishers* India

First published in India by HarperCollins *Publishers* 2025
4th Floor, Tower A, Building No. 10, DLF Cyber City,
DLF Phase II, Gurugram – 122002
www.harpercollins.co.in

2 4 6 8 10 9 7 5 3 1

Copyright © Ruskin Bond 2025

P-ISBN: 978-93-6569-352-2
E-ISBN: 978-93-6569-072-9

The views and opinions expressed in this book are the author's own
and the facts are as reported by him, and the publishers are not in any
way liable for the same.

Ruskin Bond asserts the moral right
to be identified as the author of this work.

All rights reserved. No part of this publication may be reproduced,
stored in a retrieval system, or transmitted, in any form or by
any means, electronic, mechanical, photocopying, recording or
otherwise, without the prior permission of the publishers.

Typeset in 12/16 Bembo Std at
HarperCollins *Publishers* India

Printed and bound at
Replika Press Pvt. Ltd.

This book is produced from independently certified FSC® paper to
ensure responsible forest management.

To
Rakesh
Beena
Siddharth
Shrishti
Gautam
Vaishnavi

With love and gratitude

Preface

Journals ...

I have kept them over the years, but never on a regular basis. Sometimes too much was happening, sometimes too little.

My first book, *The Room on the Roof*, was based on the journal I'd kept as a sixteen-year-old in 1951. Over the next two years it became a story, transformed into fiction. Eventually it was published as a novel.

There's no fiction in this journal. Seventy years after celebrating my room on the roof in Dehradun, I am now celebrating the window of my small bedroom-cum-study in Landour, Mussoorie.

I have slept beside this window since 1980, and I hope to spend a few more days and nights beside it before going into the great unknown.

Can a window give you stories and poems and essays and memories over a period of many years? In many ways, this one has been at the heart of my writing. It opens on to sky, clouds, sunshine and rain, all the things that keep us alive; on to hills striding away into the distance, on to trees, windswept hillsides, small houses straddling the slopes, winding roads, pathways; and below me, children on their way to school, people from nearby villages, local tradesmen, tourists (mostly in cars), dogs, mules, monkeys; and in the monsoon, mist in the valley and moths on the windowpanes.

The seasons bring their own visitors – crickets in the spring, tourists in the summer, beetles in the rains, prowling panthers in the winter. Except for occasional excursions into the wider world, I am here all year round, like the little ghost in the attic.

I can always find something to write about, and the window is my collaborator. I remember an old song, 'Can't Help Singing'. In my case, it's a question of 'Can't Help Writing'. Once there's a pen in my hand, I have to put it to some use.

It's a warm day today, but there's a cool breeze coming in at the window. It's a Sunday and cars are honking on their way to Char Dukaan (which now has six shops). They won't see the snowcapped peaks today. Too much dust from the plains, too much smoke from forest fires.

But it will clear up once it rains, and then, even with my weak eyesight, I will be able to take in the purple of the mountains, the deep blue of the sky, the bright green of new leaves on the deodars, and all the colours of life.

31 JULY

Flower of the Day: Indian Pink

'**A**lways lovely,' according to flower-lore. And when given to your sweetheart it says: 'You are always lovely.'

I shall start each day of this journal with a flower and its symbolism, traditional or just my own personal meaning.

Why? Simply because it is a nice way to start the day.

Even if there's no flower on the window ledge, there are flowers on the hillside, down in the valley, and in the greater world beyond the horizon.

Flowers are the ultimate symbol of creation. And when the last flower has faded and fallen, our world will be no more.

But this is no time to be pessimistic and melancholic. The last 'pink' of summer is still blooming on my windowsill. And right next to it I see a little green shoot coming up.

It's just a blade of grass.

But what would we do without grass? Our sheep, our cattle, our wild creatures, all depend on it. So do we, for wheat is grass; barley and maize and rice are all grass. Sugarcane is grass. Bamboo is grass, as any elephant will tell you. Most of our planet is covered with grass, except where we have replaced it with concrete. Sometimes a blade of grass will peek through the concrete as well.

Take away all the grass and we are left with an uninhabited planet.

So today I celebrate the presence of grass – so fresh and green at this time of the year, made lush by the monsoon rains. Grasslands, meadows, tall grass, short grass, sweet grass, the grass on your lawn, the grass of a desert oasis giving hope to thirsty travellers, the grass growing in an abandoned fort or palace, giving hope of nature's ability to recover and restore.

Where there is grass there is water. Where there is water there is life.

As I write, the rain begins to come down – steadily, relentlessly – drumming on the old tin roof, even making inroads through a couple of weak spots and dripping on to a pile of books and folders stacked up on a side table. I rush to their aid, cover them with a plastic sheet (plastic has its uses!) and then look for a bucket to take the steady drip from the ceiling.

This building has stood here for well over a hundred years, but sometimes it has to give way to wind and rain. When I came to live in it some fifty years ago, the rusty old tin sheets were blown away in a blizzard, and I got up at daybreak to find my blanket under a blanket of snow. The roof was repaired and strengthened.

I love watching the gentle fall of the snowflakes. But snow is cold, and I don't want it in the bedroom.

1 AUGUST

Flower of the Day: The Bean

The bean?

'My love is like a bean-field in blossom,' wrote the poet John Clare. And the bean has been a pretty flower, white or pale blue, and the long green bean is in itself an elegant thing.

It's bean-time now, up here in the hills, and the village women are busy collecting the ripe beans, while the menfolk bring them to the town for sale in the vegetable market.

Almost every day someone is at the front door, offering us a bundle of beans at a ridiculously low price. Beans, cucumbers, radishes, these are the chief products of the season, down in the villages. After the rains, there will be maize and millets; and then, nothing. For little grows in the winter months, when the grass turns yellow and the ground is hard with frost. The villagers manage with the grain they have stored away.

The beans pile up in our kitchen. Beena sends some of them down to her mother at the flat near Mullingar. We have them cooked with potatoes – *aloo-bean* – but I like them best with roast chicken and mashed potatoes. But this is Shravan, Beena's month for fasting, and she won't be preparing meat dishes for a few more days. So I must be patient and build up my appetite for chicken roast and mutton keema with green peas.

Why is it that at the age of eighty-eight, my appetite is keener than ever? Is there something wrong with me? Yesterday I had four buttered toasts for breakfast, one with marmite, one with a sandwich spread, one with garlic pickle and one with sweet mango chutney. Mysterious are the ways of the human physiology.

Shrishti – Rakesh and Beena's daughter, now twenty-five – brought a bag of plums from the village near the Yamuna where a group of local village women and she have been experimenting with different plants, fruits, herbs, etc.

The plums were very good, sweet and juicy, and I put away a few of them. Not too many, because I know from experience that too many plums can give you the runs.

When we first came to Ivy Cottage, there were plum trees growing on the open hillside above the house. Then the owner of the land removed them and built a guesthouse above us. Now we see tourists instead of plums.

Never mind, we need tourists too. At least the hill station does.

And those plum trees had gone wild, the fruit being edible only for the monkeys. But when they were in blossom, they lit up the hillside with their creamy white flowers, and I would emulate the poet by exclaiming: 'My love is like a plum tree in blossom.'

But that was a long time ago.

There isn't much blossom about at this time of the year, but the ferns are flourishing everywhere, even on the trunks of the oaks and deodars. In the winter and early summer, one has to go down to streams or shady places to see the ferns. In August, they come to see us.

2 AUGUST

Flower of the Day: Scarlet Geranium

A show-off and a bully ...

I woke up this morning after a strange dream. In it, an old friend had conspired with another writer to deprive me of some award or distinction, and I was furious about it. I went after them with a hockey stick. Fortunately I woke up before I could inflict any damage. I can't recall who the writer was, except that she was a woman and a person of influence.

Later in the day, I had a nosebleed. No connection with the dream (as far as I know) and it did not last long. It may have been due to my blood pressure being high, or the tablets I take for a skin irritation. Or anything. Or nothing.

I placed a cold wet handkerchief on the back of my neck and lay down for an hour.

I had to get up because we had visitors. Two young women in spotless white saris were sitting in the front room. They were Brahma Kumaris, women who decide to spend their lives in celibacy and don't marry. They wanted to tie a rakhi on my wrist, making me their spiritual brother.

I now have a very pretty sacred thread on my right wrist, and hopefully it will protect me from bad dreams, jealous rivals and nosebleeds.

Beena and the ladies got into a long spiritual conversation and, as I am not really the spiritual type (except where birds and flowers are concerned), I returned to my bedroom and started reading an old Rex Stout mystery that Shrishti had ordered for me online. I'm having fun going back to the Golden Age of the detective story.

Because of the nosebleed, I thought it better to do without the evening vodka and orange juice. I turned on the TV but was repelled by one of those unpleasant political debates that seem to excite everybody. Returned to Rex Stout and his fat detective, Nero Wolfe, who grew orchids on his roof and did all his detecting from an easy chair.

And so to bed ... (as Samuel Pepys once said).

3 AUGUST

Flower of the Day: Love-in-a-Mist

Legend has it that if the petals of this little flower are placed on the eyelids of someone who is asleep, the sleeper, when they awake, will fall in love with the first person or creature that they see – be it man, woman or donkey.

I'm glad no one had placed petals on my eyelids last night because the first thing I saw this morning was the face of a rhesus monkey peering at me through the windowpane. And he (she?) did not look particularly friendly.

Note to self: Must read *The Golden Ass* again. The Romans knew a thing or two about falling in love with quadrupeds.

Yesterday there was rain. Today there's a thick mist. Visibility (from my window) down to about six feet.

There is something romantic about mist, hence the name of the flower; nothing romantic about fog (a combination of mist, smoke, exhaust fumes, etc.) as every New Delhi resident knows.

The highland mists of Scotland play their part in the novels of Robert Louis Stevenson. The fogs of London lend atmosphere – sometimes sinister – to the novels of Charles Dickens: *Little Dorrit*, *Bleak House*, *Great Expectations*, *Our Mutual Friend*. They represent Victorian London. Fog is a major character in the books.

When I arrived in London in November 1957, I found myself enveloped in a thick pea-soup fog. It smelt filthy and evil. I groped my way down a busy street, bumping into people, losing my bearings, finally ending up spending half the night in a cafeteria at a bustling railway station, drinking several cups of equally unpleasant coffee. I believe the fogs of London are not so bad now; they've done something to lessen their virulence.

Give me a highland mist any day. Give me the mist of the mountains. Actually it is just a cloud, groping its way through the gaps in the hills, Presently it will rise and then we'll have more rain.

Umbrellas are opening. There was a time when all umbrellas were black. A gloomy sight. I wonder why they had to be black – it didn't make sense. Now I see coloured umbrellas: blue, yellow, pink, green, multicoloured.

There is something cheerful and optimistic about a colourful umbrella.

5 AUGUST

Flower of the Day: Honeysuckle

'A bond of love', according to the sages

A delayed birthday card (delayed in the post) from Nurse Nirmala in Ranchi.

A very special nurse, a very special person, radiating warmth and goodness.

About thirty-five years ago, I had to spend over a month in the local mission hospital after a surgery for haemorrhoids resulted in a troublesome infection. The doctor who had operated on me was young and full of enthusiasm, but lacking in experience and the skills that go with it. The hospital was also in a bad way at the time: ill-equipped, understaffed and only just surviving – like some of its patients. But there was this one nurse, a tribal girl from Ranchi, who bustled about, often doing the work of two; cheerful, friendly, the perfect nurse. Her attentions certainly helped me get better.

I recovered and came home. A few months later, I heard that the nurse had been transferred to a hospital in another part of the country.

Time passed – as the subtitles said in the silent movies. It was the winter of 2019, and I was signing books at a literary festival in Ranchi. A small bouquet of flowers was placed in front of me. I looked up. It was Nirmala. I recognized her immediately. She was a little older, a little fuller, but that glow was still there, the glow of unchanging friendship.

She was a senior matron now, and the mother of three grown children. There was no time to visit her home, which was in a village some distance from Ranchi, and the organizers of the festival had me tied up for other events. But those were happy moments, and time cannot steal them from me.

The honeysuckle binds ... but I don't see it so often now. I remember when almost every home in the hill station had a shrub or two growing against a wall or pillar, the modest flowers lending their fragrance to the sounds and sights of summer. The honeysuckle looked after itself and made no demands; maybe that's why it was neglected. And when the old houses disappeared and new and bigger houses came up, the old shrubs and climbers were buried in the builders' rubble.

When I was a child, I was told that fairies lived among the honeysuckle, feeding off their nectar. Well, a garden is a natural home for fairies, and they will find shelter almost anywhere; but there are not many blooms that lend so much sweetness to the air.

7 AUGUST

Flower of the Day: Wild Arum

Also known as 'Lords and Ladies'

Up here in the hills it's called the Snake Lily or 'Saanp ka Bhutta', its scarlet berries resembling corn on the cob. The berries are said to be poisonous – and they certainly look dangerous. But I have seen a cow munching on them without apparent aftereffects. Still, it's better not to experiment with wild berries.

Mid-monsoon is when these hooded lilies flourish. The dark green of the hillside is lit up by the presence of the bright scarlet berries.

We could do with some colour on these damp, sunless days. Scarlet berries, colourful umbrellas, a red-bottomed bulbul perched atop the streetlight pole. It's a lightless pole, the monkeys having damaged it out of sheer mischief.

Mussoorie has lost its honeysuckle, and I've lost a front tooth. It was wobbly for some time, and at lunch it came out as I was having my rajma and rice. Last month I lost an incisor. Never mind, I've still got a number of good teeth capable of dealing with a chicken croissant or a boiled carrot. But not a raw carrot!

10 AUGUST

Flower of the Day: Nettle

It stings, like the fungal infection between the thighs that has been bothering me for some time and keeping me awake at night.

Last night, at 2 a.m., I switched on the bed lamp and wrote the following nonsense verse.

You could call it 'A Painful Poem'.

> *Oh, life is just a riddle,*
> *A silly sort of fiddle,*
> *A doodle-dandy diddle,*
> *A time to laugh or cry.*
> *It's really just a muddle,*
> *A fiddle-faddle huddle,*

A paddle in a puddle,
A time to laugh or cry.
Sometimes it's all a puzzle,
A kind of jigsaw juggle,
A jig or just a bubble,
A time to laugh or cry.

I may not be much of a poet, but I think I could qualify as a rhymester.

14 AUGUST

Flower of the Day: Catmint

They say cats love catmint, and maybe that's why Mimi the cat (of Persian descent) went in search of some, having taken off through an open window.

She was missing all day and was finally discovered stuck in a rainwater culvert, where she had taken shelter from the unwelcome attention of street dogs and monkeys. Rescued, she was carried home and given a bath – and an extra helping of tuna for dinner.

There's plenty of peppermint growing on the hillside, but I must find some catmint for Mimi – or try growing it.

Another Day in Landour

A terrific cyclonic storm hit us around midnight and continued till 3 a.m. The rain got in through the old roof and flooded my bedroom. My room always gets the brunt of a storm, but when the weather is fine it's the best room, with its windows opening to the skies, the mountains, the valley.

This is a month of clouds and heavy mist, and sometimes the mist drifts in through the open window. Then it must be closed, or the moisture will get into clothes, books, bedding.

But last night the moon was out, almost at the full, and I opened the window wide to let in the moonlight and the flavours of the night.

To live in a room without a window is like being in a prison cell. The Covid problems kept us all homebound for almost two years. To have spent most of the time in a room with bare walls would have tried both body and soul. *The Count of Monte Cristo!*

For an old man who can't go out very often, the window is his lifeline to the rest of the world. As time goes by, the window increases in importance. The sky by day, the stars by night: they are always there, constant in their companionship. A ring of mountains, equally constant. The trees, the valley, a town gleaming in the sun after days of heavy rain; for some time, we are free of air pollution. And below me, the roads, and a pathway zigzagging between them. The human comedy plays itself out before my eyes.

I am fortunate, of course, in having this little eyrie, this window on the world. I lived in New Delhi once, and I did have a window, but it opened out to my neighbour's rear wall.

Even a wall can be interesting, though. There were cracks in the wall where a lizard had made its home. In the space between the wall and the roof, pigeons had made their nest. Their gentle cooing was background music to my thoughts. And during the rainy season, small plants took root in various places, and a dandelion flowered and offered me a wish.

Treacherously, I wished for a better window – and got one.

You can't suppress a dandelion. One of nature's most resilient plants. We insult it by calling it a weed.

17 AUGUST

Flower of the Day: Dandelion

It will pop up where you least expect it – on the steps of the house, on the windowsill, upon an old wall. It invites the sun to enter your home. Blow away the delicate seed-ball and make a wish ... If nothing else, your wish will have helped disseminate the seeds of the flower.

Dandelions forever!

As permanent as the dandelion are some of the books I have cherished over the years. I have loved them for the elegance of the writing, the author's personality coming through the pages, their skill with words and sentences creating a desire to revisit the book again and again.

Here are some of them:

The Story of My Heart by Richard Jefferies	(The meditations of a naturalist)
Walden by H.D. Thoreau	(The author takes to the wilderness to find meaning)
The Bird of Dawning by John Masefield	(A saga of the days of the sailing ships)
Youth, Typhoon, The Nigger of the 'Narcissus' by Joseph Conrad	(Full of the sea and its many moods)
Spin a Yarn, Sailor by 'Sinbad'	(A tramp ship's captain describes some stormy voyages; and all those wonderful sea shanties!)
Wuthering Heights by Emily Brontë	(Passion and the elements on the Yorkshire moors)
The Quest for Corvo by A.J.A. Symons	(Biography at its best – accompanying the author on his fascinating search)
Hindoo Holiday by J.R. Ackerley	(An eccentric maharaja and an equally eccentric writer)
The Diary of a Nobody by George and Weedon Grossmith	(Mr Pooter aims for the sublime and achieves the ridiculous)
A Voice Through a Cloud by Denton Welch	(A gifted young writer, severely injured in a road accident, describes his last months)

20 AUGUST

Flower of the Day: Lady's Slipper

It's a ground orchid, a small white lady's slipper treading softly through the lush monsoon grass.

Tree orchids don't grow up here – you'll have to go to Sikkim for those spectacular blooms. But we have two or three ground orchids flourishing on the hillside throughout this month.

Having some difficulty sleeping at night. The best remedy is to switch on the bed lamp and try to write something – nonsense verse or a limerick.

Last night I tried a tongue-twister, which came out like this:

Slippery slippers slither and slide as I slip swiftly on the slimy sinuous slipway.

Fell asleep at 3 a.m., counting ladies' slippers – the real ones.

23 AUGUST

Bird of the Day: Laughing Thrush

A strange, silent morning.

No cars, no horns honking, no motorbikes revving up, no traffic jam on the road below the cottage. Where have all the tourists gone?

Is the Covid virus back with a vengeance?

Has World War III broken out?

No, it's just that the heavy rain of the last two days has washed the road away, halfway down to Dehra. It will take all day to clean the mess. There are hundreds of cars stranded on either side of the landslide. Nothing will come this way till late evening.

Peace and blissful silence for a few hours.

A pair of laughing thrushes arrive on the parapet. I am seeing them after some time. As usual, they are quarrelling with each other – sound and fury signifying nothing.

I have given them names: Putin and Biden.

~

Each year is a conquest.

Every time I complete a year of my life, I feel as though it's been a victory. This has been the case ever since I got into the seventies. Before that, I didn't pay much attention to the passing of the years; they were something to which I felt entitled.

But after seventy you are not entitled to anything.

31 AUGUST

Wrote two stories last month.
Tore up one of them.
When did I last tear up a story?
Unfinished stories, many times.
But this was a completed story.
It just didn't work.

No flower of the day.

4 SEPTEMBER

Flavour of the Day: Fish and Chips

A day of mist and periods of sunshine.

The kids got me dressed, and we drove out to the Kempty area. Siddharth, Shrishti, Gautam and I. Grandfather gets an outing.

Siddharth took us to a little restaurant with a great view of the surrounding hills. We had the place to ourselves. Shrishti and I drank beer, and she sang several songs very sweetly. I sang a bit too – a sea shanty – it was my first beer in a couple of years. I ordered fish and chips. The food wasn't great, but that did not matter. It was good to be out of the house after a long period of physical inactivity. Even the traffic jams couldn't spoil our day.

Getting up the steps to the front door requires some effort now. They are the most uneven steps in all of Landour. Twenty-two of them, all uneven. Still, they discourage too many visitors.

8 SEPTEMBER

Sometimes a dream can be turned into a story (*The Enchanted Cottage*, for instance). But last night, in bed, I worked out a story about being marooned on a rock at high tide, with a girl also trapped on a neighbouring rock.

I got up, went to the loo, returned to my bed and fell asleep. Dreamt that I was similarly marooned with two small girls, and that I led them back to safety before the tide came in. The dream had a happy ending.

But the story I'm going to write will have a different ending.

Ate a jam paratha for the first time. Recommended by Siddharth and Shrishti. It consists of jam (in this case apricot jam) in a rolled-up paratha. Ugh!

Kids will eat anything these days. And I'm still experimenting.

9 SEPTEMBER

The Queen of England passed away yesterday. She was ninety-six.

I was working as a junior clerk in a grocery store in Jersey when we heard that Elizabeth's father, King George VI, had died, and that she was to ascend to the throne. George VI was a good king, who stayed in London throughout the Blitz; he was a sick man but performed all his duties with a smile.

I was in London in June 1953 when Elizabeth's coronation took place. Seventy years ago.

I was nineteen, trying to get my first novel published. Disappointed in love and in other things, I returned to India two years later. And then the book, *The Room on the Roof*, got published.

Will the monarchy continue for long, I wonder. It's unique to England. The Queen was popular, but not so the other members of the royal family.

All the same, her passing marks the end of an era. Who's left to remember lost empires?

11 SEPTEMBER

Early morning visit from a policeman-poet, a young inspector from Andhra, who presented me with a handcrafted bullock cart – quite charming – and his little book of poems. Dutifully, I had myself photographed with book and author.

I haven't read the poems yet, but I feel we must encourage policemen to write poetry; it should make them more gentle with those in their custody.

12 SEPTEMBER

Learn from the Insects ...

If you want to be taught organization, study the ants.

If you want to learn geometry, study the spider's web.

If you want to see mechanical engineering in action, study the beetle.

If you want to look at sexual reproduction, study the earthworm.

If you want to understand terror, study the mantis.

Nature does everything to perfection. Ours is a planet designed for an amalgamation of ocean and land, jungle and desert, bird and beast, ice and volcanic fire, insect and micro-organism.

Only man is an alien. A mixture of brilliance and folly, often leading to tragedy.

Now trying to escape to another planet.

18 SEPTEMBER

For months, I was plagued by a fungal infection between the thighs. Tried many creams and ointments, antihistamines, even antibiotics, all to no effect.

Then Beena applied a solution of haldi. Immediate relief. Three days of turmeric application and the infection has cleared up.

Living alone is fine when you are young, but as the years go by, the whole business of living takes its toll on the body, if not the mind, and it becomes increasingly difficult to manage without some help. Fortunate are those who have family to look after them. I am twice fortunate in having Beena and Rakesh with me, and

Siddharth, Shrishti and Gautam usually around. What more could I ask for?

Love, companionship – and always someone to help me up the steps. Probably the most tortuous flight of steps in all of Landour. Twenty-two of them!

Strangely enough, back in 1951, the steps leading up to my 'room on the roof' at the old Gresham Hotel in Dehra numbered twenty-two as well. They indicated a struggle, I think.

But it's been a good hard struggle all the way, and I've never gone under.

I think women manage better in their old age. My grandmother (Dehra granny) lived on her own for a number of years after my grandfather died. And those old spinsters, or widows, in Mussoorie – Miss Bean and others – managed quite well into their late eighties. It's the single men, or widowers, who are often quite helpless when the knees begin to give way and the eyesight dims.

We weren't really built to live too long. But life is precious, wonderful at times, and we cling to it like limpets.

23 SEPTEMBER

It's nice to have an occasional visitor, but sometimes they tire me out, especially when they come with an entourage.

The film star who brought me her childhood memoirs was a charming person, but she was accompanied by friends and relatives – eight people. My small sitting room has only one long sofa and two single sofas, one of which I usually occupy when reading, writing or just brooding – rather like Nero Wolfe, the fat detective created by Rex Stout almost a century ago (still very readable). Anyway, I did my best and smiled for a photo-op, forgetting I'd lost one of my front teeth.

After they'd gone, I spent almost an hour with a very pleasant and courteous young probationer from the Administrative Services academy, who interviewed me for their in-house journal. He got me talking until I nearly lost my voice. He's going into the Foreign Services. His friend, who accompanied him, goes into the Forest Service. Good for both services.

Shubhi Aunty ('aunty' to Beena and Rakesh, younger than me by about fifteen years, but we all call her Aunty) arrived for dinner. She brought me a strange gown from her little shop. It makes me look like a patient in a mental hospital. I shall never wear it, but bought it because no one goes to her little handicrafts shop.

I broke my rule and had a second vodka. I both needed it and deserved it.

24 SEPTEMBER

Spent all afternoon with Siddharth and my CA, working out my tax returns.
 Needed a vodka but the bottle was empty.
 Settled for a hot cocoa.
 We must learn to do without some things.
 Sometimes.
 That's a good philosophy,
 And haven't I been doing that all my life?

25 SEPTEMBER

I don't suppose kids play Snakes and Ladders anymore. Nowadays, they are into video games before they can talk.

Snakes and Ladders was a simple board game. At the throw of a dice, you could either ascend a ladder or descend down the length of a snake. Sometimes a ladder would take you almost to the finishing line, only for you to encounter a snake who brought you back to the bottom. In a way it was a preparation for life. Almost to the top, and then down to the bottom. And if you were resilient, or lucky, you worked your way back to the top again.

I suppose it's like that with most of us. The essential requirement is resilience; but that's in our nature and not on the dice.

27 SEPTEMBER

After weeks of rain, the first full day of sunshine.

Siddharth took me for a drive past the Kempty Falls, but we did not stop there — a dark, gloomy side of the mountain where the sun does not penetrate. Long rows of unappetizing dhabas, all lit within by electric bulbs at two in the afternoon.

Went back up the hill and found a sunny wayside café called On the Edge. It was literally on the edge of a cliff. We sat outside, taking in a panoramic view of the next range, dominated by Nag Tibba. It's bare on the windswept mountainside that faces us, but forested on the moist northern slopes which we don't see from here.

All the streams in spate, rushing down to meet the Aglar at the bottom of the valley, then on to the confluence with the Yamuna.

Small villages dot the slopes of Nag Tibba and the neighbouring mountains. You will find them where there is a stream or spring. On terraced fields grow rain-fed crops; also apricots and plums.

These villages have been here for hundreds of years. The hill station itself is less than two hundred years old, an excrescence that came up as a getaway place for the British sahibs and memsahibs when it got too hot in the plains. Now adopted by the Indian middle class, who come all the year round.

But during all this time it has remained isolated from the surrounding villages. Most of the hotels, restaurants and shops are owned by plains-people. Even the residential schools cater to outsiders. The villagers, still simple people, come in with their milk and vegetables, and the bigger children walk into town to attend day schools; but that's about it.

Nearly two hundred years of seclusion. Truly an excrescence.

28 SEPTEMBER

Hatred.

It starts in the mind and then it poisons the entire system – undermining its basic functions, resulting in malignancies, heart conditions, crippling diseases, sleeping disorders ...

Hatred means unhappiness, and together they poison the body and soul.

I remember Mrs H, how bitter she was, hating everybody and making trouble for them too. She died alone, without a friendly hand to help or comfort her.

I remember S, brilliant but erratic, consumed by envy for his more successful (and possibly less talented) associates. His health falling to pieces as he grew older.

And there was the Revered B, always pointing out the faults and weaknesses of others, until he lost his memory and could no longer find fault with anyone.

The Maharani of — lived into her eighties, but she was a bitter person, domineering, estranged from her children, drinking her way to oblivion.

And by contrast there was Miss Bean, quite on her own, practically penniless, but surviving into her eighties with a cheerful disposition in spite of many years of hardship and bad luck. I never heard her say a harsh word about anyone.

However, we are but humans, and sometimes it's difficult to restrain oneself when insulted, looked down upon, made to look a fool or called an ass – even if one *is* a bit of an ass. When I was young, I reacted quite violently to insults. In my first job in Jersey, I was a messenger boy of sorts for a chain of grocery stores. The uneducated youth who was my senior kept calling me 'muttonhead' or 'asshole' or similar epithets, until I gave him a vicious kick on the shin, which had him limping for a few days. I have no doubt he hated me even more after that.

Today, if someone came up to me and called me an asshole or worse, I would probably laugh it off. Why get into a kicking contest unless you happen to be Ronaldo or Messi?

There have been one or two occasions in my life when I have been swindled out of large sums of money. Somehow, this did not make me angry enough to hate. Rather, it saddened me, because it amounted to a betrayal of trust – and revealed a certain naiveté on my part: because I am, I suppose, too trusting.

But such occasions have been rare. I have, on the whole, been fortunate in my friends, associates, employers, publishers.

Maybe the gods have a soft spot for me.

1 OCTOBER

Scent of the Day: Pine Trees

Another lovely sunny morning. Siddharth took me for a drive along the road to Thatyur.

From here, on the northern slopes, you cannot see Mussoorie or Dehra or any largely inhabited area. Just village dwellings dotting the landscape. We are in a fold of the hills, a fold of varying shades of green. About a thousand feet lower than Mussoorie, the dominant tree is the pine, with walnuts and apricots growing in the village groves.

We ate at a wayside restaurant. A vegetable thali was served almost immediately. Dal, a vegetable dish, some paneer and as many rotis as we could consume. The best roadside meals are made with vegetables fresh from the fields.

On our way back, a heavy mist came over the mountain. That will be the pattern over the next few days – sunny mornings, misty afternoons.

3 OCTOBER

My publishers tell me that my new books are selling well all over the country. Nice, to be producing bestsellers at this age! I think I'm entitled to boast a little. But only in private.

4 OCTOBER

Flavour of the Day: Pumpkin

End of the nine-day Navaratri fast.

Beena takes absolutely nothing for all nine days, just the occasional cup of tea. The rest of the family is on a partial fast (one meal a day).

I have two meals, but pure vegetarian. I miss my fried egg at breakfast. But tomorrow I shall have two.

Some local children came in for puris, channa and pumpkin sabzi. I rather like pumpkin done this way, with plenty of spices.

Pumpkin has its merits. It makes a good sweet too – the delectable petha, and also a halwa.

And a full, large pumpkin, glistening in the sun, is a most beautiful object: perfectly symmetrical, a work of art!

But in America they disfigure it, scooping out the insides and turning it into a Halloween lantern.

7 OCTOBER

Gloomy day.

But I finished a little story, 'The Girl on the Rock'.

Halfway through I wanted to tear it up (imperfect writer that I am), but then I thought, 'I've given life to something, I cannot now deprive it of a free run, even if it's only a lame thing.'

Sometimes a weak story survives even if it lacks technical ingenuity. If it touches the heart, that's all that really matters. Some of my earliest stories from the 1950s (Deoli, Shamli, those train stories!) are still around because they were spontaneous, plotless, going nowhere in particular but at the same time going everywhere – the outpourings of a free spirit.

But I should take more trouble over structure and design. When I was in Delhi in the 1960s I discovered a travel book, or journal, that was 'different' from the conventional. It was called *Hindoo Holiday* and had been published in the 1930s. Its author, J.R. Ackerley, was now the literary editor of *The Listener*, a magazine published by the BBC.

I wrote to Ackerley, he replied, and we kept up a lively correspondence over the years. I told him about the difficulties I'd had with my second novel (*Vagrants in the Valley*) and that I'd eventually abandoned it. I don't have his letter with me now, but I remember a line from it: 'Failed creations are sad, lame things.' He urged me to go back to the novel and rewrite it.

Well, I did something of the sort, and even got it published, but it was still a weak and wobbly child, although not without a certain charm.

We should never completely abandon a child (or a work) just because it hasn't quite come up to expectations.

9 OCTOBER

Here comes the sun!

The scarlet geranium on the windowsill opens its petals to welcome it.

Mimi the cat basks in a patch of sunlight on the bedroom floor. When the patch moves, she moves with it.

I can hear crickets singing. Or have I developed tinnitus?

I hear some sounds better than others. Car horns, in particular.

13 OCTOBER

Some respite from the cold unseasonal rain. December has replaced October.

About ten days ago, twenty-seven climbers (trained mountaineers) perished in an avalanche while scaling a peak in the Uttarkashi region. They were young people from different parts of the country who had paid for an extreme mountaineering course. What should have been an adventure turned into a tragedy.

I can't help feeling that the end of the monsoon (late September, early October) is hardly the time to be climbing mountain peaks. Fresh snow upon old snow can have unpredictable results. But 'adventure tourism' is the in thing (as well as other forms of tourism) and everything is done in a hurry, as though time and money are running out.

As they probably are.

17 OCTOBER

Flavours of the Day: Sounds of the Sea, the Smell of Salt on the Sea Breeze

Thought-pictures. I suppose that's the word that best describes them: those daytime visions of the past, or wishful pictures of the future.

Our earliest memories are enshrined in these thought-pictures. The Balachadi beach in Jamnagar when I was three or four. Walking along the long jetty with my mother. Taking a short cruise on an Arab dhow with my father. How terrified I was of the swaying and lurching of the sailing vessel.

I was a nervous boy. When a local aviator (one of the princes) offered to take my mother and me for a pleasure flight in his Tiger Moth, I refused to get into the plane. My mother went up alone.

But she was afraid of buffaloes. Taking a shortcut across a dried-up lake, we were followed by a herd of buffaloes. They seemed quite harmless to me. But my mother grabbed me by the hand and made me run, convinced that they were about to chase us.

These memories come back to me as pictures, and of course they never vary; they are fixed in some corner of the brain.

19 OCTOBER

Flavour of the Day: Mutton Kofta
(If you can get it!)

One of my publishers took me out to lunch in Dehradun. We went to one of the best restaurants.

'What's your favourite dish?' asked my host.

'Kofta curry,' I responded without hesitation, remembering the delicious kofta curries that Granny's khansama used to make.

So we ordered kofta curry.

The koftas turned out to be made of vegetables, or some sort of suet. I was very disappointed but could hardly complain.

'Are you enjoying your koftas?' asked my host.

'Delicious!' I said.

We have to be philosophical about life's disappointments.

But what happened to real koftas, those tender meatballs?

Someone tells me you can still get them in Kashmir!

22 OCTOBER

The 1940s and 1950s were, for me, the years of railway travel, and many of my early stories happened in trains or on railway platforms. 'Romance brought up the nine-fifteen,' wrote Rudyard Kipling, and there was still an element of romance about steam engines and epic railway journeys.

It was the small stations, lonely in the wilderness, that appealed to me the most, and I wrote little stories around romantic encounters, such as 'Night Train at Deoli', 'Time Stops at Shamli', 'The Woman on Platform 8' and others. Things happened during railway journeys in a way that they don't happen on a bus trip or air travel. An airport is a busy place, but arid and without character. A railway station has a life of its own, and no two stations are alike.

Deoli was really Kansrao, a tiny two-roomed station in the forest between Raiwala and Dehradun. Only one train stopped there; all the others rushed through with a great deal of chugging and blowing and whistling. Then the forest would be silent again.

The station master did not have much to do except keep the elephants off the track. If there was a collision the elephant usually got the worst of it, although on one occasion an entire train was derailed, with several casualties. Elephants and train engines are still on a collision course.

Platform 8, on the other hand, was in Ambala station, a busy junction with several platforms. And Kalka, a little further on, was where I transferred to the small narrow-gauge hill train or railcar, which was swifter and more comfortable.

Halfway to Shimla, we would stop at Barog before entering a mile-long tunnel. Barog was well-known for its breakfasts, and I remember having breakfast there with my father – it was, in fact, the last time that I saw him; a few months later, one of my teachers had the painful task of breaking the news to me that he 'had gone to his Maker'. Painful for the teacher, devastating for a nine-year-old. But life carried on. And so do the trains.

26 OCTOBER

Woke up wondering why crickets and cicadas were in full cry at this time of the year. Crickets one might hear around now, but not cicadas.

Then realized there was a ringing sound in my ears, unrelated to insect orchestration. Possibly the aftermath of two nights of hearing firecrackers going off on the road and rockets whistling past the window.

Looked up the symptoms in my old (pre-1940) medical dictionary. Persistent ringing and buzzing in the ears is apparently a symptom of tinnitus.

I love some of these medical terms. Tinnitus. Makes me feel like the Tin Man in *The Wizard of Oz*.

I presume we get parrot fever from parrots, but can we get chicken pox from chickens?

If Santa Claus is stuck in a chimney he's sure to get claustrophobia.

Bad joke ...

When I was nineteen, living on my own in London, I picked up a rare eye disease called Eale's Disease. Was Eale the doctor who discovered it? Or was he the first patient to be diagnosed with it?

Or was Eale simply a misspelling of 'eel'?

I do think it had something to do with eels, because that was what I was seeing – tiny wriggling eels obscuring the vision in my right eye. The eye surgeon I went to was fascinated by my condition, had powerful photographs taken of my retina (almost blinding me in the process) and wrote an article on the subject for a British medical journal.

A course of cortisone injections cleared up the condition (cortisone was the new medical marvel in those days), but it recurs from time to time, usually when I'm in low spirits or poor health. Rest and plenty of sunshine usually put the eels to sleep. And if that doesn't work, two fingers of vodka (taken with guava juice) will knock them out.

31 OCTOBER

Last night, over a hundred and fifty people perished as an old suspension bridge collapsed in Morbi in Gujarat. It was getting dark, and as they fell into the swirling waters of the river, their despairing cries could be heard as they plunged towards their unforeseen and abrupt departure from this life. And then, silence.

The survivors could thank the gods, or their stars, for their deliverance. There had been over four hundred of them on that shaky old bridge. One step forward and you were lost. One step backward and you were safe. The whims of chance.

What had brought them there in the first place? The desire of the individual to be part of the crowd, to belong to the surge of the crowd. And then destiny takes over.

The humble perish, the mighty fall. Old bridges give you no warning.

Earthquakes make no distinction. The first rumble and we are rushing for safety and the great outdoors, lest the houses we have built so carefully collapse upon us. Fear strengthens our resolve to escape. But none of us can escape fear, even if the resulting panic is only there for a few seconds. And then, obliteration.

In South Korea, a day ago, a similar tragedy. Too many people in a confined space. People fall, are crushed to death as others panic and tumble over them. In such situations it's everyone for themselves. The drowning man will drown his rescuer!

What were so many people doing on that narrow street? Celebrating Halloween! I didn't know it was a festival observed in Korea. An American import. But anything for a party!

Overloaded boats capsize midstream. Wedding tents go up in flames. Football stadiums erupt with violence. Humans, like lemurs, gravitate towards the place where others gravitate. Life isn't about rewards and punishments, it's about consequences.

2 NOVEMBER

Flavour of the Day: Blackcurrant Jam with Creamy White Butter on Toast
(That means I'm feeling good.)

Amazon has named me its Author of the Month for November. So I'm not a has-been just yet, though some would like me to be one.

Enjoyed watching Hitchcock's first 'suspense' film, a silent made in 1927, loosely based on Mrs Belloc Lowndes's novella *The Lodger*. Ivor Novello expresses every emotion with his beautiful melancholy eyes. In those early silent films actors had to act with their eyes, and close-ups were all-important. Pleasant to watch a film without the heavily accented dialogue of 'talking pictures'.

But it wasn't really silent. A brooding, repetitive musical score ran right through the film; must have been added on later.

Hitchcock gives the film a happy ending – not in the book. He did the same with *Suspicion*, which rather spoilt it.

One of his best was *Strangers on a Train*, based on a brilliant psychological thriller by Patricia Highsmith.

Highsmith write some very unsettling and disturbing crime novels – *The Talented Mr Ripley* and *Deep Water* among others – the best 'crime' writer of the generation. More in tune with today's readership and the current obsession with damaged human beings.

7 NOVEMBER

Rakesh and Beena took me down to Dehra to have my eyes examined, as I hadn't been seeing too well for a few months.

Amritsar Eye Clinic, run very efficiently. Dr Devesh Sharma examined me, as did a number of assistants and technicians, all very sweet and friendly people.

It seems I have glaucoma in one eye and cataract in the other (or in both?). Anyway, I am on various eye drops for the present. Hate the prospect of any kind of surgery!

Missed out on lunch but put away a number of pakodas made at the old pakoda stall halfway up the hill. It's been in the same family since I was a kid. Famous for its pakodas. What would we do without pakodas? Can't imagine an India without pakodas!

We drove back after dark. I'm glad I can't drive. Confronted by blinding headlights all the way. Day trippers on their way down. Hundreds of pairs of flashing headlights. Don't know how Rakesh manages, but we were home in an hour.

19 NOVEMBER

Are cooks happy people? They seem to be a well-adjusted lot.

Siddharth seems to be happiest when he is preparing something for himself and for others to consume. I have watched him preparing momos – giving his undivided attention to each one, fashioning and filling each dumpling with loving care. He whistles as he works. Other problems seem to disappear.

But then, cooking is a hobby for him. Do professional full-time cooks get the same pleasure out of their work? It must get monotonous at times, preparing meals two or three times a day, not for family or friends but for strangers.

I'm no cook. Boiling an egg is as far as I go. But I suppose writing a story is rather like cooking an interesting dish. You need the basic ingredients – a theme or storyline – and then you make it appetizing with appealing characters and incidents. If the story comes off, it's like a successful biryani. Or shepherd's pie. If it flops, it's a failed omelette.

Conundrum: Why do dogs go round in circles before they sit down?
Gautam: We'd have to ask them, I suppose.

20 NOVEMBER

The world's population has now crossed eight billion. We have been generous in our contribution to this massive achievement.

I'm not complaining. I like people, most people anyway. Humans are the only animal that smile, apart from the Cheshire cat.

People can love, they can hate. They can create and they can (and do) destroy. And I'm one of them.

But more and more people means more sewage running into our rivers, more plastic finding its way to the sea, more garbage piling up in and around our cities. And the planet's green cover diminishing rapidly. Future generations must suffer for the sins of the present generation. Just look at the sort of leadership the world has had to put up with in recent years – the egomaniac Trump; the destroyer of his own habitat, Bolsonaro in Brazil; the mindless Putin; Johnson partying as Britain flounders; the fatuous in North Korea; the strongman of Burma – the list is a long one.

∼

Dirge

(To the tune of 'Where Have All the Young Men Gone?')

> *Where has all the garbage gone?*
> *Into your green fields, my son.*
> *Where has all the plastic gone?*
> *Into our great ocean, son.*
> *And where has all the sewage gone?*
> *Into our great rivers, son.*
> *We're doing our best for you, dear one,*
> *The road to hell is almost done.*

One must not be too pessimistic, though. The human species seems to thrive in pollution. And it's the tendency of nations to go to war with each other that will probably end up depopulating the planet one day.

24 NOVEMBER

Never having gone out of my way to mingle with the literary set, I don't know many authors. Most of them are driven by their egos. Back in the 1950s I was approached by a writer called G.V. Desani, who asked me to nominate him for the Nobel Prize. He had a nomination form that he was carrying around, asking other writers to recommend him as well. I'd read his novel, *All About H. Hatterr*, which was quite funny, and I obliged him with my signature. He never wrote another book, and I don't know what happened to him.

Some years ago, a part-time journalist came to me with a similar nomination request. He'd published a few articles in newspapers. To get rid of him I signed the form. Then I said, 'Now why don't you recommend me for the Nobel Prize?'

He looked at me in astonishment. Could there possibly be other writers, apart from him, who were worthy of such an honour? Impossible! He was the one and only ...

No wonder vanity publishers do such good business.

3 DECEMBER

Couldn't write for a few days due to an attack of gout in my right wrist, which made holding a pen rather painful. Various painkillers did not help.

'Avoid tomatoes!' said a kind visitor. 'Avoid spinach!'

I promised to do both, though I like tomato sauce on my fried egg.

'Someone has put his or her nazar on you,' said Beena, naming one or two possible suspects. The evil eye!

Finally got relief from massage with an oil we had picked up in Bhutan many years ago.

And what a lovely trip that was! Roses, sunflowers, verdant valleys. Not too many people. Just good people. May it always be like that.

7 DECEMBER

Clear skies for over a month.

At 6.30 a.m., I get up to watch the dawn break: the finest moment of the day as the eastern sky glows red, then bright orange, then apricot, all merging into daylight. Almost an hour later the sun comes up over the mountains, and shafts of sunlight pour through the window, illuminating the pad on which I am writing.

I can't write for long because of a painful wrist, but I felt I had to record these moments.

To change the words of an old poem slightly: 'The night has a thousand eyes and the day but one, but the light of a million lives is the rising sun.'

15 DECEMBER

I am intrigued by temperatures the world over. Right now it's -10 degrees Celsius in Winnipeg, Canada. How can people live in such extreme cold, and why should they? Give me Honolulu at about 30 degrees all the year round. Or St Helena at 21 degrees. What was Napoleon complaining about? Better than Paris at this time of the year.

Islands intrigue me. Port Stanley, in the Falklands, is 13 degrees today, warmer than Britain at 4 degrees. Of course it's summer down there. Warmer than Mussoorie last night! I like Tenerife and Gibraltar and Madagascar, all islands with sensible temperatures.

16 DECEMBER

The warm dry spell suits the plants in my small sunroom. The geraniums flaunt their scarlet and deep pink blooms, and the poinsettia has revived and turned into its own unique shade of red.

Geraniums give you different shades of colour all the year round. And poinsettias brighten up these winter days.

Geraniums do well in hill stations and in plateaus (like Bangalore) where the climate is mild. The hot drying winds of Delhi don't suit them; nor do cold winds. Up here, they like the afternoon sun, out of the wind.

So do I.

Granny had geraniums on the veranda in Dehra. She said their aroma (from the stems not the blooms) kept the snakes away. I mentioned this in one of my articles long ago and a well-known expert on snakes wrote to the paper saying that snakes did not have a sense of smell. I'm sure he was right, but how do we determine a reptile's sense of smell? Is there some way of measuring it?

Me to Gautam: Do snakes have a sense of smell?
Gautam: We'll have to ask them.

17 DECEMBER

Kind lady sent me a hamper of vegan food, no doubt trying to convert me to veganism. Most of the items, made to look appetizing, were made from soya, which I hate. I tried a biscuit, which tasted like mud, sweetened a little.

Vegans are noble people who limit their diets to plant life. I can do without meat (have done so for long periods) but it would be hardship to go without butter (I love butter!), cheese, eggs (scrambled with milk), and strawberries or bananas with cream.

Mimi, our cat, has the ideal diet. A little milk, a little cream. Sometimes fish. Sometimes chicken. An occasional chocolate.

I offered her a soya biscuit. She sniffed at it, then turned away in disgust.

Nature knows best. Eskimos can't live on lettuce, and rabbits can't live on seal fat.

I must have been a cat in some former life – a well-spoilt, well-fed cat, as worshipped by the ancient Egyptians. Those people knew a lot of things we don't!

1 JANUARY

Fish today!

A good way to start the new year.

After quite some time, Beena made fish curry for lunch. River fish, of course. A large fish with something resembling a long moustache. I forget the name. No, I remember. The singhara, caught in the upper reaches of the Jumna. Very tasty. Must have more fish this year.

P.G. Wodehouse's character Jeeves, the valet who was always getting his master Bertie Wooster out of trouble, put his brainwaves down to a diet rich in fish. Well, Jeeves is fictional, but I know of a great many Bengali writers who thrived on hilsa, a freshwater fish with a delicate flavour. And didn't Shakespeare fish in the Avon, Mark Twain in the Mississippi and Thoreau in Walden Pond? Freshwater fish, of course. Sea fish is for seafarers.

So we'll make this the Year of the Fish. My journal, which has been flagging, will pick up, and my rhymes will acquire a fresh edge.

In the little Aglar river behind Mussoorie, the common fish is a small mountain trout, very tasty but full of tiny bones (rather like the hilsa), so you can't just gulp it down – you could get a fish bone stuck in your gullet. (The remedy for this is to eat some soft bread; it will carry the bone away.)

I don't care much for sea fish, although some of my favourite writers have been seafarers – Joseph Conrad, R.L. Stevenson, W.W. Jacobs. But I like to think that whenever they reached a port, they treated themselves to river fish.

Some memorable novels about rivers:

Huckleberry Finn by Mark Twain

Three Men in a Boat by Jerome K. Jerome

The River by Rumer Godden

The River of Stars by Henry de Vere Stacpoole

Heart of Darkness by Joseph Conrad

9 JANUARY

Joshimath, the small temple town on the way to Badrinath, has been sinking, and sinking fast. Residents are having to flee from their homes as floors open up and walls topple over. Too much roadbuilding and tunnelling for various power projects has taken its toll on a fragile mountain.

And here, Landour bazaar is also showing a tendency to slip off the narrow strip of mountain to which it clings. Cracks in the road widen and the old buildings teeter – some houses have seen floors added to their structures over the years. This narrow link between Mussoorie and Landour, almost two hundred years old, was meant for pedestrians and ponies, but now must support the weight of hundreds of vehicles transporting tourists to upper

Landour. Even hill stations have their expiry date, and some have gone past it.

And not only hill stations. There were seven cities of Delhi before the present city of New Delhi. What remains of them? A few old tombs, some crumbling battlements and city walls.

Nothing built by man lasts forever. And there's a limit to what a ravaged hillside can hold up.

12 JANUARY

I spent a few hours in Joshimath a few years ago, but all I can remember of the place is an ancient mulberry tree which they called the Kalp-Vriksha, a tree of immortality. It wasn't very tall but it had a huge circumference, and it took me about twenty strides to circumvent it. I hope it's still standing.

We should protect and venerate our old trees. So many fine old banyans have been destroyed because they take up space that is coveted by humans. Dehradun was once famous for the great variety of its trees, many propagated in the early days of the Forest Research Institute. Now few remain.

13 JANUARY

Let's celebrate our trees,
Let's honour them.
They've been with us for centuries.
That mighty oak upon the hill,
Its branches green and supple still,
The great deodar still standing tall,
An old walnut leans against my wall.
And down below, across the land,
The banyan spread its friendly hand.
For centuries some trees have stood,
Through drought and storm and annual flood.
They give us shelter, help us breathe,
And cater to our every need.
Let's celebrate the old trees now,

Place garlands on each tender bough,
Let's honour them and give them space,
And praise their goodness and their grace.

(Written on an impulse this Friday morning.)

19 JANUARY

Finally, overcast skies and the promise of rain or snow.

Shrishti is recovering after a sudden attack of painful abdominal spasms. Our local hospital treated her for gastritis, but to no avail. Rakesh and Beena took her down to the big hospital in Dehra, where an ultrasound detected a stone in the kidney. Fortunately, it passed into her urinary tract, and she came home yesterday in her natural good spirits. Grateful to the Almighty and all who helped her. A little prayer helps too.

20 JANUARY

Shubhadarshini came over in the evening and we put on YouTube and listened to some of my favourite Eartha Kitt songs: 'Santa Baby', 'Under the Bridges of Paris' and 'I Want to Be Evil'. I was in London in 1954 when Eartha Kitt first exploded on the musical scene. I travelled to a suburban cinema to see her in *New Faces*. Some of the best films get shown outside the West End.

The family loves watching the Garhwali song-and-dance programmes. These are an appealing blend of folk and Bollywood. The girls are beautiful, every one of them, especially in their colourful costumes. The men dance well too. And the choreography is excellent.

Shubhadarshini (Shubhi Aunty to the kids) is an adventurous and independent person in her late sixties who occasionally goes off into the mountains in search of snow leopards or Abominable Snowmen. She did see a snow leopard once, but the Snowman has remained elusive. Allergic to milk, she is now a vegan of sorts, but a meat-eating vegan, if there can be such a thing. Perhaps we can call her a non-veg vegan. Anyway, I gave her all the vegan products given to me by the kind lady last month.

She had brought me a packet of Mars bars, knowing I had a weakness for nougat and caramel fillings.

She left at ten, a little tipsy.

And so to bed, with my hot-water bottle.

31 JANUARY

A long cold spell and the gout in my writing hand made writing difficult for some time. This morning there's a little warmth in the sun, and I'm the better for it. There's nothing like the sun!

Saw a couple of crows – jungle crows – after a long interval, probably a year. We used to see many crows, raucous and cheeky, on the hillside, but they have all gone. Our garbage dumps, especially down in Dehra, are possibly too toxic now even for them.

1 FEBRUARY

Yesterday two crows, today two monkeys at my window. Does that signify anything? I'd rather it had been two sparrows or two bulbuls. Anyway, I offered the monkeys a banana. One of them snatched it from me, and they both took off. Not a word of thanks! At least a crow says 'Caw' by way of thanks whenever I give it some of my toast.

Rakesh and Beena took Prem (Rakesh's father) down to Dehra: his vision is severely impaired, probably due to his diabetes.

Shrishti made a nice salad for lunch – tomatoes, onions, salt, coriander and lemon in olive oil. She learnt to make it when she was in Russia, on an educational trip, about five years ago. Not really a Russian salad. Better, in fact.

The sunroom was really warm today. The geraniums are loving it, flaunting their colourful flower-heads.

Mimi has occupied my chair. She likes cushions. A spoilt cat, and she knows it.

I sit on a tin trunk. I jump up again. It's hot!

6 FEBRUARY

Maidenhair. My favourite fern.

I opened an old diary and a long-pressed maidenhair fell out. It had lost its colour, but otherwise it was perfectly preserved, fronds as delicate and pretty as ever, the stems still firm, dark against my open palm. I remember plucking it near a small spring near Hathi Paon, many years ago.

The maidenhair likes some sun, but will flourish only in the presence of running water – a spring, a dripping rock face, the banks of a small canal. Its name (according to an old herbal) is so given because the dark slender intertwining stems resemble the pubic hair of a young woman. A delightful comparison. But that isn't why I like it. The fern isn't easy to locate, and I like its rarity and fresh appearance – ever fresh, as long as its thirst is quenched.

When I was a small boy in Dehra, I was familiar with a clump of maidenhair just where the little canal appeared from its underground passage into the light of day. That was the canal that came down from Rajpur, went underground near the Dilaram bazaar and emerged at the end of the Old Survey Road, not far from Granny's house. The canal, which lent a certain character to the town, was covered over (or done away with, I'm not sure which) when the roads were widened a few years ago, to accommodate the menacing traffic of the town, now a state capital.

The canal also serviced the many gardens and orchards that were a feature of the town in its early days. Now the old bungalows and spacious compounds are hard to find; the apartment blocks have taken over. The litchi gardens have been replaced by shopping malls. Such is progress.

As I write, news comes in that thousands have perished in a massive earthquake in Turkey and Syria. Hundreds of thousands have been rendered homeless, their houses and high-rises in ruins. The forces of nature remind us that we are not the arbiters of everything that happens on this planet. We are obsessed with space exploration, knowing little of what exists and what happens beneath the earth's crust. Wars and geographical boundaries pale into insignificance when the earth moves, the volcanoes erupt, the tidal waves sweep in. Then we are no more masters of the earth than the rabbit quivering in its burrow.

I return the maidenhair to the pages of the old diary.

12 FEBRUARY

Glorying in the warmth of my sunroom, I felt something slip down my neck and move about on my back. An insect perhaps, or a dry leaf. As it continued its explorations, I decided to investigate and asked Beena and Vaishnavi (Shrishti's cousin) to lift up my sweater, shirt and vest. They did so. Both screamed.

A small terrified lizard fell out with a plop and scuttled away to the safety of the geranium pots. Luckily for Bill the lizard (named after the one in *Alice in Wonderland*) Mimi wasn't in the room. It was only a skink, quite harmless (I think); they have taken up residence among the geraniums.

Said Beena: 'You're always writing about birds and beasts. Now they want to sleep with you.'

14 FEBRUARY

Some rain, enough to make one shiver, but it's been a long dry winter.

16 FEBRUARY

There are some books that pulsate with the writer's love for a place or its people, or some special attribute.

I think of H.E. Bates's love for the English countryside, so ardent in his Uncle Silas stories, *Alexander*, and other country tales. Of William Saroyan in *My Name Is Aram*, celebrating his boyhood and Armenian background. Of Rumer Godden in *The River*, describing the Bengal countryside with love and nostalgia. Of Richard Jefferies in *The Story of My Heart*, so passionate about every growing thing. Of Conrad in *Youth*, celebrating a young man's first wonderful sea voyage. Of the traveller Freya Stark, writing about the desert. And the poets John Clare, Robert Frost and Walter de la Mare, celebrating the green world.

18 FEBRUARY

We live in awe of the things that are bigger than us – the sun, the stars, the oceans, the mountains, the fires beneath the earth's surface – but we don't hesitate to harass and exploit the creatures of the world: trading in elephants' tusks, rhinos' horns, the body parts of tigers, bears, pangolins, whales, seals – and we don't hesitate to destroy their habitats too.

But when the volcano erupts, we flee; when the tidal wave comes, we run; when the hurricane blows, we dive for cover. Then we are no superior to the ants and beetles.

In fact, the ants manage better on these occasions.

20 FEBRUARY

It's been unusually warm during the past week. Last night, I found a moth on the windowpane. An indication of an early summer and probably a hot one.

Shrishti made a cold coffee with vanilla ice cream. Most refreshing.

Whenever she makes something different, she tries it out on me.

This was followed up by a strawberry milkshake – with real strawberries, lots of them. Delicious.

Somehow, I didn't care so much for the guava-on-toast.

27 FEBRUARY

I'm one of those people who likes to start the day with a newspaper. It's just habit, of course. After all, most of the news is depressing – wars, economic woes, hate speeches, rapes, murders, natural disasters, climate change, financial scams, unemployment, racism: hardly an inspiring way of starting the day.

But it's better than the TV news channels and their pursuit of the sensational and controversial. They thrive on the assumption that the average viewer is a cretin, a person of low intelligence, who will swallow all their prejudice and bombast. And they are probably right.

So I take three newspapers and hopefully get a balanced view of all that's happening in our great wide beautiful world.

But I wish they would do away with those full-page ads, which get in the way of the news pages. Can't they place them at the back of the paper, after the sports pages?

Mimi knows how to deal with those superfluous pages. She sharpens her claws on them and then rips them apart, thus enabling me to see the headlines.

The newspaper habit goes back to my childhood in Jamnagar. My father took *The Statesman* and early in the morning, the newspaper boy would ride over on his bicycle and call out 'Chappa!' – which means newspaper in Gujarati. The paper would land on the veranda steps and I would go out to retrieve it and hand it to my father – that is, if he wasn't busy beating up some creamy white butter for breakfast.

I was five and too small to take an interest in the news reports, although I do remember reading about a German bomb falling on Buckingham Palace. But on Sundays there was a children's page, and I devoured it. I liked comics too, especially the funny ones; the American superheroes only came my way when I went to boarding school.

I was sixteen and just out of school when I started sending my stories to newspapers and magazines. Those early efforts were dispatched like missiles and came back like torpedoes! But in August 1951 I did have a story accepted and published in *The Illustrated Weekly of India*, the country's leading family magazine. It wasn't much of a story, just a sketch about a schoolmaster, but it brought me a cheque for thirty rupees, my first earnings from my pen.

7 MARCH

Holi comes and goes quietly, until nature decides to lend a hand. The clouds burst and the hail rattles noisily on the roof. As it melts, it finds its way through roof and ceiling and – splash! – it's on my face and pillow, and I have to leap out of bed. All hands on deck!

I dry out near the heater and make this entry. Writing has been painful recently because of my weakened wrist. Is it gout or something else? Putting pen to paper is painful.

Seventy years of writing has damaged my sword-hand.

8 MARCH

The ninety years of my life can roughly be divided into three parts.

1934–40, Jamnagar, on the Kathiawar coast, for the first six years of my life.

Then periods in Granny's house in Dehradun, and two years with my father in a Royal Air Force hutment in New Delhi (1941–43). Eight years in boarding school in Shimla (1943–50) interspersed with winter holidays in Dehra after my father's passing.

Four years in Jersey and London (1951–55), described in *Scenes from a Writer's Life* and *Lone Fox Dancing*.

Returned to India in March 1955 as the mango trees came into blossom. *The Room on the Roof* published in 1956.

Freelanced from Dehra, then to New Delhi in 1958. Worked there 1959–63, then fled to the hills.

(End of part one.)

∼

1964–94, most of the time in Mussoorie, with occasional change of residence. First eight years in Maplewood Lodge, near an oak-and-maple forest with a stream at the bottom of the hill. This period gave me 'The Angry River', 'The Blue Umbrella', 'Panther's Moon', 'The Tunnel' and many other stories.

When a road was built through, the property moved uphill to Landour and I rented the upper flat of Ivy Cottage in 1980. By then Rakesh was seven, going to school. Wrote several children's stories including 'The Cherry Tree' and 'Getting Granny's Glasses' in the 1980s – now bestsellers in India.

(End of part two.)

∼

1994 to present: Children grow up. Rakesh marries. Siddharth, Shrishti, Gautam, all born in Ivy Cottage. Flat now ours.

Books multiply. Era of lit fests.

16 MARCH

Shrishti down to Dehra to stay with Shubhi Aunty, who has been admitted to a heart clinic with breathing difficulties. Apparently her heart is functioning at just 20 per cent of its capability. Or so we are informed.

Siddharth arrives with another cat. Black mask and black ears. Batman! Or rather, Bat-cat.

Mimi very angry. Off her food. Sulking. Being 'catty'.

'Goodbye' is apparently short for 'God be with you'. We live and learn.

19 MARCH

Now Mimi occupies one floor and Bat the other. Conflict averted. They even have separate potties. They use them too. No messing up the house. World leaders, take note.

Beena brought home a basket of strawberries. The fattest, juiciest strawberries I've ever enjoyed. Strawberry fields forever!

Hailstorm. The hail collected on the roof, melted slowly, worked its way through roof and ceiling and dripped on to my face and pillow just like last time. Got me up in the middle of the night.

I placed a bucket over my pillow, sat in front of the heater and read *The Consolation of Philosophy* for an hour. But philosophy was of no help. Turned to a biography of Edgar Allen Poe. So gloomy that it actually cheered me up.

22 MARCH

After four days of rain, the sun came out. It's still cold, but there's a feeling of spring in the air. A sprightly, refreshing feeling.

It's time to celebrate the coming of spring. Shakespeare celebrated it ('Sweet lovers love the spring'), so did Kalidasa (in *Shakuntala*). And so did the Chinese poets and Japanese haiku poets. So did painters and musicians and dancers the world over – in calypso beats, flamenco flourishes, or with Bharatanatyam eyes, hands and feet.

All nature celebrates the spring. The birds love it. Parrots come screaming, 'It's spring, it's spring!' Wild geese stream northwards, honking away in the sky. The peacock spreads its dazzling plumage. Doves coo, thrushes warble, bulbuls whistle, finches twitter, magpies chuckle, mynahs squabble. Crickets sing in the grass. Grasshoppers join in. Cicadas tune up their violins. Earthworms turn in their soft muddy beds.

Where would we be without earthworms to till our soil? A barren planet. While giving thanks to the bees and butterflies for fertilizing our plant life, don't forget the earthworms, working underground. And luckily for us, they have active sex lives, as any biologist will tell you.

Whether squirming worm or turtledove,
Spring is the time for making love.

That's me, not Shakespeare.

And what's it all about, oh great Librarian? We are here today and gone tomorrow.

A little love, a little kiss, and if you're lucky, some spicy malabari curried fish.

Ah, sweet mystery of life.

5 APRIL

I have always maintained that when I've run out of ideas or something to write about, I have only to look out of my window to see something that merits a few lines, or even a page or two, or sometimes a story.

Well, it was a dull morning, and the muse was still asleep, so I opened the window in expectation of some new revelation. And what did I find? Fog! Impenetrable fog. Couldn't see a thing. The road, the mountains, the valley, all gone!

I closed the window with a sigh of resignation. Nature always has the last laugh.

Later, I found a small skink hiding in the rubber plant. It did, at least, inspire a nonsense verse.

> *Oh! For the life of a skink*
> *It's better than taking to drink*
> *But when taking a nap*
> *Beware of the cat*
> *Or she'll finish you off in a wink.*

Mimi and Bat-cat were in the roof garden, though, stalking a butterfly who was too smart for them.

A snail on the window ledge. Must have lost its way.

> *Oh! For the life of a snail*
> *Better than going to jail*
> *But beware of the French*
> *Or they can have you for lunch*
> *Served up in a gilded pail.*

17 APRIL

The last three afternoons were given up to writing a short story, 'The Night Has a Thousand Eyes' (the opening lines of a remembered poem – it makes a good title) in which I recall the two-week voyage home from England to Bombay in 1955.

I've turned it into a romantic tale. Of course it wasn't like that. But the ship itself – a Polish liner called the *Batory* – was real. Something or the other was always going wrong with it – sailors deserted it, fires broke out, people fell overboard … I wonder what happened to it finally.

Returning to Dehra in March of that year, with my novel finally accepted by Andre Deutsch, I set out to make a precarious living as a freelancer, bombarding every newspaper and magazine in the land with stories and articles. Just managed to get by. Then moved to New Delhi in 1958. That's another story.

Received a letter and a book of poems from an eighty-year-old retired engineer living in Roorkee. He tells me that he started writing poetry at the age of eighty. They are in Hindi, so it will be an effort to read them, but I must write and congratulate him.

I receive many letters from schoolchildren. Can't reply to all of them, but if there's a particularly nice one I send the writer one of my paperbacks, with an encouraging message.

Warming up. Nice hot sun. Wrist not so painful now.

20 APRIL

Early memories – Jamnagar in the 1930s.

My father beating up a bowl of cream to make the delicious white butter that I still prefer to other butters.

Sorting stamps with him. He was an avid collector.

Crossing a dried-up lake on foot with my mother and being chased by a herd of buffaloes.

Panicking as I was about to be taken for a ride in a small biplane. Panicking as I was about to be taken for a trip in an Arab dhow. I was a nervous child.

Hated haircuts. Kicked and screamed. Had to be rolled up in a sheet so that the barber could cut my hair.

Stung by bees as I came down from the roof, disturbing their hive, which had been built into the stairs. Father bathed my inflamed arms and legs with a solution of potassium permanganate.

The old palace had a room at the top and coloured glass windowpanes. I loved looking through them. Many years later they went into my story 'The Room of Many Colours'.

Balachadi beach. Collecting seashells. Paddling in the shallows.

Going to the pictures with my parents. English-language films came but seldom. But we saw *Tarzan the Ape Man* (Johnny Weissmuller) and Noël Coward's *Bitter Sweet*. These were the first films I saw.

My first book was a big book of nursery rhymes that included the poem about John Gilpin's runaway horse, which was hilarious. Then a battered copy of *Alice in Wonderland*. And I loved comics – the funny ones.

Cosmos flowers grew rampant on the lawn. I wandered among them, imagining I was in a forest.

The ruler of the state (the 'Jam Sahib') gave us lots of toys at Christmas. I came last in a race organized for the children of the staff.

Frogs everywhere during the rains. Snakes swallowing frogs. Saw a snake in the bathroom. It was thrown out by a servant, but I wouldn't enter the bathroom for several days, preferring to remain constipated.

Attended a cricket match. (Jamnagar was famous for its cricket, being the state of Ranjitsinhji and Duleepsinhji.) Sweets were constantly passed around, and I did not pay any attention to the cricket.

We left Jamnagar in 1940, when I was six. World War II had broken out, and my father had joined the RAF.

These memories came rushing back on a chilly April afternoon in Landour, after an interval of eighty years. Faces in the mist.

29 APRIL

Thought is free.

Isn't that wonderful? We have to pay for everything else, but there is no tax on what we think.

Our thoughts are free to roam wherever they wish, and no one can hinder them. Lie awake thinking, or spend an entire afternoon in thought: there is no rationing of your thoughts, no limitations.

We can be made to pay for whatever we say, what we write, what we do, but there are no restraints on what we think. Our thoughts are ours and ours alone. No one can take them from us.

5 MAY

Dreams are free too. No charge. And while you can't control the dreams you experience when asleep, you have complete control over your 'daydreams', which are your thoughts running rampant through your mind.

Daydream as much as you like. No one can stop you. It's our sleep-dreams that are really interesting, though, because they bring so many variables together – people from the past intermingling with people from the present, and complete strangers turning up and taking centre stage.

Freud and others wrote a lot about dreams and their meaning, and there was a time when I used to record my dreams in a 'dream book'. But honestly I find them quite meaningless, although pleasant at times – even memorable. Those can be attractive, intriguing. But some dreams can be unpleasant too, and we force ourselves to wake up.

There was that dream in which I heard someone knocking on the front door, late at night. I got up, went to the door and opened it, to be confronted by a woman about eight feet tall and dressed all in black, her face only partly visible. She tried to come in, but I pushed her back and bolted the door. She kept knocking on the glass until I woke up.

7 MAY

The cold wave continues. I can't remember the month of May being so cold and wet. And yet there's all this talk about the world getting warmer. Would that some of that warmth would come this way.

I sit by the electric heater. The cats are occupying the most comfortable chairs. Rakesh and Beena are in bed. Outside there's a heavy mist. I don't hear any birds, but maybe that's because there's a constant buzzing in my ears. I can hear the car horns all right, though. There's no escaping them.

In the UK, King Charles III is crowned with some ceremony. Poor old king, I feel sorry for him. It must be lonely being the last known king in the world. And with his younger son always snapping at him like a spoilt terrier.

12 MAY

Some of these dieticians and fitness enthusiasts are fanatical know-alls.

I was sitting in the foyer of the Savoy when a woman approached me and, without a word of introduction, told me I should drink a glass of lime juice every day. I thanked her for her advice and said that I did take my evening vodka with lime juice or guava juice, but that too much lime juice on its own aggravates my gout.

She then changed tack and told me I should drink two glasses of milk every day. I told her that I hated milk, had hated it since I was a child, but was happy to increase my intake of ice creams and milkshakes to make up for any deficiency of milk.

She gave me up for a gone case and strode off, looking for another victim. She was a skinny woman in her forties, probably envious of all my fat.

14 MAY

My birthday is now looming, and a small group of boys (and two teachers) from my old school (Bishop Cotton in Shimla) came to see me to record my memories of school life. I was at Bishop Cotton in the 1940s, when a lot was happening in the country and the world: World War II, India's independence, Partition, Gandhi's assassination, Chandigarh coming up (it wasn't there in 1950 when I left school).

I kept them entertained for nearly two hours and before they left they sang 'Happy Birthday, Mr Bond'.

16 MAY

Someone's catty remarks were relayed to me. The tongue is the most destructive weapon in the world. It can break up friendships, families, communities, nations. It can even bring about wars.

Beware the tongue!

17 MAY

Wonderful dream. In full colour too!

I was walking over a verdant and unspoilt mountain, full of all kinds of trees, shrubs, wildflowers and beautiful pheasants that were twice the size of ordinary pheasants. A rocky hillside draped in yellow primroses. Shades of green everywhere. I walked on and on, crossing one range after another, getting further and further away from home ... until I woke up, feeling refreshed – forest-refreshed.

26 MAY

The birthday celebrations (on 19 May) went off well.

Cambridge Book Depot put on a good show with a monster cake that fed about a hundred youngsters.

Spent evening at home with family.

Did interviews with several newspapers and one (via Zoom) with the beautiful and well-read actress Sonali Bendre.

A visit from Shobhaa Dé and family; she fixed up an interview with *The Times of India*.

Three books were released last week, including *The Golden Years*.

A plenitude of cakes. I don't want to see another. I'm beginning to look like Miss Havisham's wedding cake in *Great Expectations*.

What did I say in my interviews? That to stop working was to stop living. And that I was a philosophical person rather than a spiritual one, and that I would rather contemplate a lotus than meditate in a lotus position. The latter gives me a horrible cramp.

Thunderstorms. A cold and windy May.

And so to bed …

28 MAY

Letter from a 'fan':

'I read one of your books when I was at school. I forget its name. It had a blue cover.'

8 JUNE

Swollen and painful left foot. Gout, probably. Or an oedema due to something else.

Our family homeopath Dr Atul looked me over and promised some relief with his powder. He is a good soul who likes to sit and chat with Beena for an hour or two, interpreting her dreams.

He asked me to choose a number between 1 and 60, and I said 59. But he did not elaborate on this exercise.

Wrote a few limericks. This is good therapy when I feel a little low. Here's one:

There was a handsome young actor
(God's gift, I'm told, to Max Factor)
But he proved to be lax
In paying income tax
And he ended up driving a tractor.

I hasten to add that I do not know of any ex-actors driving tractors.

18 JUNE

Writing about my boyhood, I find that it's my visual memory that's good. Everything comes back to me in pictures – the house we lived in, the roads, gardens, cinema, individuals like Dhuki the gardener, crippled Miss Kellner with the biscuit tin, Granny's enema can hanging on the veranda wall, the little canal, the maidenhair fern growing beside it, the tonga ponies trotting down the road, the jackfruit tree, Granny's false teeth resting in a mug of water, the ostrich egg on the mantlepiece (where did that come from?), a vase full of sweet peas, fish cutlets for dinner, swinging on the garden gate ...

Those are Dehra memories. And then there are Delhi memories and Jamnagar memories and Shimla memories

– endless memories going back to the 1940s – all in the form of pictures. Conversations are forgotten and even the situations, but those pictures from the past are clearer than ever. Early memories only seem to improve as I age.

20 JUNE

Most of the family away for their annual village puja.

Looked after wonderfully well by Shrishti. She didn't leave the house for the entire week. Made sure I had everything I needed – and more.

Last night, stayed up till midnight watching old Mr Bean shorts. I'm rather like him, I fear.

Family returns. Mimi happy to see Rakesh, to whom she is much attached. She rolled about in ecstasy. Was sulking while he was away. Who says cats don't show emotion?

21 JUNE

Made a special effort to go out and meet Mr Mehra senior (of Rupa Publications) for lunch at the Savoy. Shrishti accompanied me.

Roadblocks and traffic meant that it took us nearly two hours to get there (it's normally a twenty-minute drive). We joined a long line of cars crawling up the hill in slow motion. I have to admire the patience of these people, determined to go where they had set out for and to see what they planned to, no matter how daunting and uncomfortable the journey. And what do they get at Kempty? A waterfall and pond choked with plastic waste. To which they add more plastic by way of water bottles and fast-food packaging.

Someone said we need more hill stations. To further devastate the environment, no doubt.

Civic leaders are celebrating 200 years of Mussoorie's existence. They forget that before the British built houses on this mountain, there was a village here called Kulri. The town's centre is still called Kulri. So why aren't we celebrating Kulri instead of Mussoorie? A colonial hang-up!

30 JUNE

As Mimi and Bat-cat were constantly fighting, we gave the latter to a friend in Dehradun who has four cats and two dogs. Obviously, he has lots of garden space.

Bat-cat seems to have settled down, and we thought Mimi would be pleased to have the house to herself again. But she began looking for him all over the house, making strange noises all the time. It seems she misses him now. No one to fight with!

Like humans, cats need enemies. We hate them when they are around, we miss them when they're gone. Peace doesn't come naturally to man or beast.

1 JULY

Over 600 mules died due to exhaustion,
  Carrying pilgrims to Kedarnath.
  May the mules be born again as men,
  And their owners born again as mules.

4 JULY

Probably the hardest part of writing is getting to work in the morning (or in the afternoon, or at night) when that blank page stares you in the face and challenges you to fill it with meaningful words and sentences.

Some writers create various devices to help them start off the day's work.

Hemingway would sharpen twenty pencils – and then start typing.

Willa Cather would read a passage from the Bible – not because it would put her in touch with the Supreme Being, but because it put her in touch with great prose.

Dickens would go for a long early-morning walk.

J.B. Priestly would light his pipe.

T.S. Eliot would converse with his cats.

As I don't belong to such distinguished company, I'll keep my methods to myself, except to say that the earlier you start, the more you will accomplish.

6 JULY

Style maketh the writer.

I think of all those great writers who cultivated their own individual style – in America you had Dorothy Parker, Truman Capote, William Saroyan, Damon Runyon, Raymond Chandler, Ernest Hemingway, Gertrude Stein and, of course, Mark Twain.

There is perhaps more formality in the style of British writers, although one can hardly accuse Shakespeare of formality. And Sterne went out of his way to break all the rules.

Dickens was a great creator of memorable 'scenes' – Mr Micawber declaiming on the economics of happiness; the runaway David Copperfield being received by his aunt, Betsy Trotwood; Mr Pickwick on the ice; Pip encountering the escaped convict ... Sometimes he overdid it, was carried away by his enthusiasm for a dramatic moment, but those 'scenes', once read, are never forgotten. No wonder so many of his novels were turned into outstanding films.

10 JULY

Seashells.

They bring back childhood memories. A five- or six-year-old, I wandered about on the sandy Balachadi beach near Jamnagar. My parents were close by, but I liked to be on my own, searching for seashells washed up on the beach. Those little shells, the empty, discarded homes of little sea creatures who lived out their lives on the bed of the ocean, while we were living ours on dry land.

Well, I was no philosopher then – but I loved the shape, variety and natural beauty of those shells, and I still keep a few.

11 JULY

Lady Luck doesn't come our way very often. Her visits are rare and fleeting. We must make the most of them, cherish her presence, make her want to come again.

Bad luck, on the other hand, doesn't like having to go away. He's like an uninvited, unwanted guest, lingering on, refusing to leave, making everyone's lives miserable. We must throw courtesy to the winds and throw this unwelcome visitor out of the home, out of our lives, refuse to admit him again.

Patience. When all is still, good luck will come again.

13 JULY

A love of books is the best insurance against old age.

When younger members of the family are busy and unable to give all their time to us, we can go to our well-filled bookshelves, find an old friend or make a new one and spend hours in their company, forgetting our disabilities and the loss of physical pleasures.

As time goes on, we have to live within our own minds, and what better way to do it than to enter the minds of those who have tales to tell and something to say about the lives of others?

Even a good dictionary can be fascinating because there is much to learn from words and their associations.

15 JULY

'Pursue your passion.'

I heard someone say this just yesterday morning. He wasn't a writer, or an artist, or a musician. He was a racing-car driver.

I saw him on TV, and he was telling an interviewer just how he felt after winning a gruelling and hazardous car race. He felt wonderful. It was the culmination of his boyhood dreams.

From his childhood he'd wanted to be at the wheel of a racing car, travelling at 200 miles an hour. He'd been racing for years and now he was finally at the top, amongst the world's most famous drivers. His passion took him there … passion and ambition and dedication.

But passion by itself isn't enough. It must be backed by the honing of our skills and the aim for perfection. Be you a violinist or an athlete or an architect or a racing-car driver, you must aim for perfection. We fall short, of course. But the striving for perfection does often result in excellence and even glory.

18 JULY

I suppose we can divide the world into two kinds of people: givers and takers.

Look back on your life and make a list of those who gave freely, and those who took greedily.

I'm afraid the takers would make a longer list; but as long as there are a few givers, the world won't be too abysmal a place.

20 JULY

The sword is not the weapon, the gun is not the weapon, the bomb is not the weapon, the nuclear device is not the weapon.

The only weapon is man.

He wields the sword, he fashions the bullet, he pulls the trigger, he primes the bomb, he creates the desire that destroys everything.

22 JULY

One lone sparrow on my windowsill – and even he or she looks malnourished.

There was a time when flocks of sparrows would congregate on the road below. Every house had its sparrows. The country, the world, was full of them.

So what happened to them? Were they wiped out by all the chemicals that are sprayed in the fields to kill the weevils and other pests that bore into the plants we eat? Little birds and other small creatures succumb to pesticides too.

Or is it something else? Something in the atmosphere, something in the air we breathe, that is wiping out small creatures, and may one day wipe out big creatures, even humans. Another virus, probably manmade, insinuating itself into our daily lives and turning all of us into helpless sparrows …

24 JULY

'And the rain it raineth …'

It rained all night. In the morning, when I opened the window, the mist flowed into my room.

A good time for writing, I suppose. There's not much else one can do, apart from studying bank statements.

Two days ago the skies were clear, and we drove out to a spot on the Thatyur Road, where the hills open out to provide a panoramic view of the next mountain. No one about, except for an ancient-looking villager taking his afternoon walk, one studied step at a time. He didn't falter. I walked faster but kept tripping up. Have I forgotten how to walk? The Covid pandemic has kept me housebound for such a long time; and while my mind remains active – and my writing pads full of my handwriting – my legs have gone to sleep!

26 JULY

The rains are over, and the horse chestnuts are falling.

The ferns have turned a russet brown and yellow. But not the maidenhair which, tucked away in a shady corner where there is a perpetual drip of spring water, retains its verdant freshness. But you have to look for it.

Nature goes about its business quietly, with that wonderful skill which millions of years have perfected.

There is perfection in green growing things, even a blade of grass.

It is rare in human beings who lack grace, amongst other qualities. We are rather like ants, industrious and ambitious, building anthills that sooner or later become heritage sites.

28 JULY

'I write for myself and for strangers.'

So said Gertrude Stein, a writer who went to great lengths to make her writing as obscure as possible, almost as though she wanted her readers to remain strangers.

Most writers write for themselves, because if you can't please yourself, you will please no one. And the reader who comes to your work for the first time is, of course, a total stranger. But if he or she likes your writing and wants more of it, they will become a friend, albeit an unseen one.

And the best of readers remain unseen.

You don't want someone looking over your shoulder as you write.

31 JULY

After the age of eighty, every day is a bonus.

So, savour the moment, make it count.

Soak in the sunshine and, if it's cloudy, admire the cloud patterns; if it rains, take a deep breath and take in the cool clean air and the scent of the earth – for it too must breathe.

Read a little, write a little. Listen to music. Take a short walk. And if walking is difficult, go for a drive.

If you can't do that, open the window and look at the birds, the trees, the cats, the dogs, the mules, the monkeys … look at the people, no two of them the same.

Will we see them again? Will we come this way again? Who knows?

Acknowledgements

My thanks to Udayan Mitra, Amrita Mukerji, Mugdha Sadhwani and rest of the team at HarperCollins for their work on this book.

About the Author

Ruskin Bond is one of India's most well-known writers. Born in Kasauli, Himachal Pradesh, in 1934, he grew up in Jamnagar, Dehradun and Shimla. In the course of a writing career spanning over seventy years, he has published over a hundred books, including short-story collections, poetry, novels, essays, memoirs and journals, and edited anthologies and books for children. *The Room on the Roof* was his first novel, written when he was seventeen. It received the John Llewellyn Rhys Memorial Prize in 1957. He has also received many other awards, including the Sahitya Akademi award in 1992, the Padma Shri in 1999 and the Padma Bhushan in 2014. Many of his stories and novellas including *The Blue Umbrella*, *A Flight of Pigeons* and *Susanna's Seven Husbands* have been adapted into films.

About the Author

Ruskin lives in Landour, Mussoorie. His other books with HarperCollins include *These are a Few of My Favourite Things*, *Koki's Song*, *The Enchanted Cottage*, *Build Your English Skills*, *How to Be a Writer*, *How to Live Your Life* and *The Golden Years*.

Ruskin Bond is eighty-nine years old: long past sixty, the age at which one becomes a senior citizen; also the age around which it is said one should think of retiring from active life. He takes great joy in the world outside his window: the changing shades of nature, interesting people, good food, nice walks. Inside his room there are thoughts and memories, and the journal and letters he writes every day.

All of it makes for a wonderful life – and that is what this book is about. In his trademark warm, witty, whimsical style and his marvellously simple prose, Ruskin tells us how to enjoy the advancing years some of us are blessed with, and how to make the most of the amazing gift called life.

HarperCollins *Publishers* India

At HarperCollins India, we believe in telling the best stories and finding the widest readership for our books in every format possible. We started publishing in 1992; a great deal has changed since then, but what has remained constant is the passion with which our authors write their books, the love with which readers receive them, and the sheer joy and excitement that we as publishers feel in being a part of the publishing process.

Over the years, we've had the pleasure of publishing some of the finest writing from the subcontinent and around the world, including several award-winning titles and some of the biggest bestsellers in India's publishing history. But nothing has meant more to us than the fact that millions of people have read the books we published, and that somewhere, a book of ours might have made a difference.

As we look to the future, we go back to that one word— a word which has been a driving force for us all these years.

Read.